Pips in Pots

Written by Alison Hawes
Photographs by Steve Lumb

Collins

Cut it.

Get a pip.

2

pips

Get a pot.

Go and get the mud.

Pop the mud in the pot.

Dig a pit in the mud.

Pick up a pip.

8

Pop it in the pot.

Top up the mud in the pot.

Pat the mud in the pot.

Get a can and tip it on the pot.

Set the pot in the sun.

Pips in pots

pips

14

pot

mud

can

Ideas for reading

Written by Clare Dowdall, PhD
Lecturer and Primary Literacy Consultant

Learning objectives: read simple words by sounding out and blending the phonemes all through the word from left to right; read some high frequency words; read a range of familiar and common words and simple sentences independently; show an understanding of how information can be found in non-fiction texts to answer questions about where, who, why and how; use talk to organise, sequence and clarify thinking, ideas, feelings and events; use phonic knowledge to write simple regular words and make phonetically plausible attempts at more complex words

Curriculum links: Knowledge and Understanding of the World: Ask questions about why things happen and how things work

Focus phonemes: p, o, t, s, c, u, g, e, i, a, m, d, ck, n

Fast words: the, go

Word count: 63

Getting started

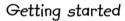

- Using phoneme flashcards, display the high frequency words *a, in, and, up, on* and practise quick-reading them.

- Practise blending a selection of words from the book, e.g. *cut, mud, pick, pat* – check that children understand the meanings.

- Look at the front and back covers of the book. Name the objects that are shown *pot, soil, trowel.* Discuss what the girl is doing in the pictures.

- Look carefully at the title and read it together. Using magnetic letters build the word *p-i-p-s* and practise blending the sounds. Repeat with *p-o-t-s.*

Reading and responding

- Hand out the books and ask the children to read them from beginning to end, taking time to look at the pictures.

- Move around the group, listening to them blending through words independently, praising their blending and fluent reading.